HOCKEY HEROES

The Game's Great Players

BY GEORGE SULLIVAN

ILLUSTRATED BY DOM LUPO

GARRARD PUBLISHING COMPANY

CHAMPAIGN, ILLINOIS

Sports Consultant:

COLONEL RED REEDER

West Point athlete, coach, and for 20 years
Assistant Director of Athletics,
United States Military Academy

Photo credits:

Bill Eppridge, LIFE Magazine © Time Inc.: p. 35
Bobby Hull Enterprises: p. 11, 17, 41
Arthur Rickerby, LIFE Magazine © Time Inc.: p. 6–7, 14, 38 (top)
The New York Times: p. 26
United Press International: p. 4, 33, 38 (bottom), 66, 71, 81,
    84, 86, 89, 90, 94
Wide World: p. 8, 42

Contents

Hockey's Greatest Stars

The National Hockey League, with teams in both the United States and Canada, is the only major league in professional ice hockey. It first began play in 1917. Since that time the sport has produced hundreds of star players.

This book tells the story of three of them—Bobby Hull, Howie Morenz, and Maurice Richard.

Hockey experts consider these three to be the greatest of the greats. Each was blessed with strength and speed and the

ability to shoot with deadly accuracy. Record books give evidence of their extraordinary skills.

But each of these players was given a quality beyond skill—the ability to arouse breathless excitement, to bring a crowd to its feet screaming. Such natural showmanship is a rare gift.

Today professional hockey is more popular than ever before in its history. Almost every big city in the United States and Canada has its own team. Spectators attend games in record numbers. Millions watch on television. The success of the sport owes much to Bobby Hull, Howie Morenz, and Maurice Richard.

Bobby Hull,
the Golden Jet

It was a bright May morning in 1959. The telephone rang in the office of Tommy Ivan, the general manager of the Chicago Black Hawks.

On the line was Murray "Muzz" Patrick, general manager of the New York Rangers.

"I've got a deal for you," Patrick said.

"Good," Ivan answered, "let me hear it."

"We'll give you Bathgate and Gadsby for Litzenberger and Hull," proposed Patrick.

Most hockey fans would have been shocked to hear such a proposal. Andy Bathgate, the Rangers' right wing, had just been named the league's Most Valuable Player. And Bill Gadsby was one of the best defensemen in the game, a member of the league's All-Star team. How could Patrick possibly give up this pair?

What was even more incredible was the small "price" that Patrick was asking. Eddie Litzenberger, a center, was known as a solid player but not in a class with either Bathgate or Gadsby.

As for Bobby Hull, then twenty years old, he had been with the Black Hawks for two seasons. But most observers felt he had not shown standout skills.

Tommy Ivan was too smart to take the bait, however.

"Nice try, Muzz," he said. "But you know better than to ask for Bobby Hull. I wouldn't give you Hull for your whole Ranger team, even if you threw in Madison Square Garden."

To hockey experts like Patrick and Ivan, Bobby Hull was something special. They knew that one day he would be a great player. It was simply a matter of time.

By his third season with the Black Hawks, that time had come. Hull began to make hockey headlines.

Eighteen-year-old Bobby Hull (center) was part of the Chicago Black Hawks' "million dollar line."

In December 1959 he rang up three "hat tricks" in three weeks. A "hat trick" is scoring three goals in one game. The next February Hull scored four goals in one game.

Going into the final game of the season, Bobby trailed Bronco Horvath, 79 to 80 points, in the race for the league scoring title. A player gets one point for each goal and one point for each assist.

The final game pitted the Black Hawks against Bronco's team, the Boston Bruins.

"Let's help Bronco win this," Coach Milt Schmidt of Boston told his Bruins before the game. "Don't let Hull touch the puck. If he doesn't get the puck, he won't get any points."

Coach Rudy Pilous of Chicago also had instructions for his Black Hawks. "When one of you comes up with the puck, get it to Bobby," he said. "Let him shoot."

In the second period Hull banged a fierce backhand shot into the Boston net for his 39th goal of the year. Now Hull and Horvath were tied at 80 points.

In the third period Hull rifled a shot toward the goal. It struck a teammate's skate, then bounced into the net, counting as a goal for the team but as an assist for Bobby.

Now he had 81 points, and he won the league's scoring title for the 1959–1960 season.

Bobby Hull was just beginning though. Throughout the 1960's, he ranked as hockey's No. 1 scorer.

Bobby's favorite shot was the slap shot. He would raise his stick high in back of his body, then swing through in much the same way that a golfer hits the ball from a tee or the turf.

Hull's slap shot was the fastest one in

hockey. It was timed at 118 miles per hour, 19 miles an hour faster than the fastest pitch ever recorded in baseball.

Goalkeepers are rated as the bravest men in sports, but Bobby's whizzing shot is said to frighten the pads off some of the league's goalies. "I'm not afraid it might go by me," confessed one of them. "I'm afraid it might go *through* me."

Superstar Bobby Hull, the strongest and speediest player in hockey, goes into action.

Bobby was also the fastest man in hockey when carrying the puck. He was once timed at 29.4 miles per hour, a rate much faster than a man can run.

Bobby had more than a hard shot and high speed. To many people he was the most exciting player in hockey. "When Hull has the puck and is skating down the ice, you *know* something is going to happen," a sports writer once said.

Hull was the very image of a sports hero. Strong, square, and handsome, he had clear blue eyes and wavy blond hair. He smiled easily. He was the idol of young fans everywhere.

Bobby Hull was born on January 3, 1939, in Point Anne, a small Canadian town about 100 miles east of Toronto. Bobby's sister, Judy, once said the town's population is "about 1,000 if you count the dogs and about 500 if you don't."

Point Anne is located on the Bay of Quinte. The local youngsters could skate both on the bay and on rinks in town.

Bobby was four years old when he got his first taste of skating. Two of his sisters, Maxine and Laura, took him to an outdoor rink near their home. They laced on his skates and stood him on the ice. Almost from the first moment, Bobby skated alone.

Young Bobby went back to the rink whenever he could. He would get up at five o'clock in the morning, build a fire, put on the kettle for "porridge," and skate before going to school.

Bobby never had to take any muscle-building exercises. When he was eight, he started going into the forest with his grandfather to chop down trees for firewood. He always walked to and from school, two miles each way. During the

Ice skating came as easily as walking to Canadian boys like Bobby Hull (right) and his friends.

winter he sometimes shoveled snow from morning until night.

His boyhood offered him still another advantage as background for his career. Bobby's father had been a good hockey player and taught his young son fundamentals of the game.

One thing he emphasized with Bobby was puck control. Bobby learned it so well that, even as a little boy, whizzing across the ice, the puck stayed glued to his stick.

Hockey in Bobby's boyhood days was often a wild free-for-all. Sometimes as many as 20 boys were on a team.

With so many boys swirling over the ice, a player could not risk a pass to a teammate. An enemy player was likely to get it.

18

So the idea was to get the puck and rush the net alone. As a result Bobby developed the bad hockey habit of "flying solo" for a goal in his very earliest years.

Bobby played center on a team in a Bantam league when he was ten years old. He was strong and fast. He shot hard and skillfully enough to foil the best goalkeepers.

His bad "solo" habit became more serious. He saw no reason to correct it. "If I can take the puck and score," he thought, "why should I bother to pass?"

His coach did not try to change Bobby's habit because the coach wanted the team to win games. If winning meant letting Bobby "hog the puck," he didn't care.

When Bobby was thirteen, Bob Wilson, a scout for the Chicago Black Hawks, saw him play. He was amazed that a boy so young could be such a polished player.

Mr. Wilson spoke to Bobby's father. He obtained permission to put Bobby's name on the "negotiation list." That meant Bobby was to be kept "on the shelf" for the Black Hawks until they wanted him.

In spite of his bad habit, Bobby went up the hockey ladder very quickly. When he was sixteen years old, he was playing in a Junior "A" amateur league. Junior "A" competition in Canada is the best there is outside of professional hockey. Bobby played center for a team in St. Catherines, a hockey-mad city in Ontario province.

St. Catherines is about 200 miles from Point Anne. This meant that Bobby had to board with a family in St. Catherines and attend school there. His parents went to see him play every weekend.

Bobby's bad habit became obvious to the St. Catherines fans. "Hey, Hull," they often yelled, "are you married to that puck?"

One night before a game, the coach called Bobby aside. "A center is supposed to pass to his wingman," the coach said. "No matter how many times I tell you to pass, you won't." Bobby just shrugged.

"You're not going to be our center any longer," the coach continued. "I'm changing you to the left wing position."

This news angered Bobby. He felt that the center's position belonged to him. He and the coach argued bitterly.

Bobby's play lost its speed and accuracy, for his mind was on his resentment. He was suspended for what the coach called "indifferent play." Bobby packed up his belongings and went home.

Bobby's father refused to sympathize with him. "Life will seldom be just the way you want it," one of Bobby's friends told him. "You've got to learn to bend a little."

Bobby thought over this advice. He decided to try to "bend a little."

He went back to the team. He and the coach talked things over, and the coach decided to give Bobby back his job as the team's center.

Bobby's change in attitude had a dramatic effect upon his play. In the 1956–1957 season, with 33 goals and 28 assists in 52 games, he was scoring leader of the St. Catherines team.

Bobby returned home for summer vacation. Then in the fall he rejoined the St. Catherines team at training camp. He expected to play for St. Catherines all season.

But one September night Bobby received a telephone call from Bob Wilson. The Black Hawks were playing an exhibition game with the New York Rangers at the St. Catherines rink. "We'd like you to play with the Black Hawks," Mr. Wilson said.

Bobby ate his dinner in a rush and dashed over to the rink. He scored two goals that night. After the game he signed a contract to play for the Black Hawks. Bobby was only eighteen, and the second youngest player ever to join the National Hockey League.

Hull's first year with the Black Hawks was not brilliant. The older, wiser players of the league bounced him around. He went six games without getting a goal. When he finally did score, it was plain luck.

The Black Hawks were playing the Boston Bruins. There was a scramble in front of the net. Bobby swerved so sharply that he fell down on top of the puck, then slid into the net with the puck beneath him.

It counted just as much as if Bobby had banged in the puck with his stick. But it is one goal in which Bobby takes no pride.

Now that he was with the Black Hawks,

Bobby was becoming more of a team man. He passed much more often. Even when he scored goals himself, he was not happy if his team failed to win.

Toward the end of Bobby's second year with the Black Hawks, the Chicago coach convinced Bobby he could help the team by becoming the left wing. Bobby agreed to give up his post at center. He had learned to "bend a little."

The other members of Hull's attacking line were Red Hay, who took over as center, and Murray Balfour, the right wing. Hay was a genius at controlling the puck. Balfour was the "digger," who went and got the puck when it was deep in enemy territory. Hull was the shooter.

After Bobby won the league scoring title in the 1959–1960 season, he became a favorite target for enemy players. The more a player scores in hockey, the harder his

A Ranger player, in hot pursuit, pins Hull to the
boards and then, with a teammate, closes in.

opponents work to stop him. Bobby's body
suffered uncounted cuts and bruises, and
he lost some teeth. He learned to accept
rough play as part of the job.

His philosophy was tested during the
Stanley Cup playoffs in 1963, when the
Black Hawks faced the Detroit Red Wings
in a "best-of-seven" series. In the first

game Bobby scored two goals and the Black Hawks won.

The second game was different. Bobby got the puck. He was about to pass when a Detroit player whirled around suddenly. His stick swatted Bobby square in the nose. "It sounded like a rifle shot," one player remembers. Bobby's nose was not simply broken; it was shattered.

Bobby fell to his knees. Blood spattered the ice. His teammates quickly helped him to the dressing room.

The team doctor looked at Bobby grimly. "I've never seen anything like this in my life," he said. "You're going to the hospital."

"But that means I'll miss the playoffs," Bobby objected.

"Your health must come first," the doctor replied.

Bobby spent the night in the hospital and went home the next day. He watched the third game of the playoffs on television. The Black Hawks lost.

Bobby was heartsick. He knew the team needed him. He desperately wanted to play.

He called the team doctor and said that he was going to Detroit for the next game.

"You're crazy!" the doctor said. But he knew it was useless to try and stop Bobby.

Bobby's teammates welcomed him back. They saw nothing unusual about his wanting to play. Hockey players seldom allow mere injuries to keep them on the bench.

That night the usually handsome Hull was not a pretty sight when he went out onto the ice. His nose was covered with thick bandaging. His eyes were black and blue and almost swollen shut.

But he scored a goal. And he scored again the next night, although the Red Wings won to take a 3–2 lead in the series.

In the sixth game Bobby was a demon.

Detroit scored; then Bobby scored. Detroit got another goal; then Hull got another.

The Red Wings scored a third time. So did Hull.

In the end, Detroit won, 7–4. But Bobby, with three goals and one assist, had put on a breath-taking display of skill—and courage.

Like every great player, Hull has had "shadows" assigned to prevent him from getting the puck and scoring.

Ron Stewart of the New York Rangers often served as one of Bobby's shadows.

"Hull is the toughest man I ever played against," Stewart said. "If you take your eyes off of him for only a split second, he's gone."

Different shadows used different methods. Some followed the rule book; others didn't. "Hull is hooked, held, and tripped more than any man in the league," said Tommy

Ivan. During his first few seasons in the National Hockey League, Bobby ignored such abuse. He was so mild-mannered that in the 1964–1965 season he was awarded the Lady Byng Trophy as the league's most gentlemanly player.

That year his total of goals fell to 39. In a previous year his total had been 50.

One night late in the 1964–1965 season, Bill Reay, coach of the Black Hawks, had a talk with Bobby about his "nice guy" attitude.

"You've got to start defending yourself," Reay said. "Too many players are taking advantage of you."

The next season was different. While Bobby never started trouble, he never failed to give back as much punishment as he received. Enemy players suddenly learned to have far greater respect for him. Bobby did not win the Lady Byng Trophy that year or ever again. Instead he set a new season record for scoring goals.

The record of 50 goals was established by Maurice Richard of the Montreal Canadiens in the 1944–1945 season. The record stood for years and years. Nobody was able to top it. Bernie "Boom Boom" Geoffrion tied the mark in the 1960–1961 season. And the next season Hull himself got 50. But getting 51 seemed impossible.

In the 1965–1966 season, Hull rang up his 50th goal in the 57th game. There were thirteen games left on the schedule. Surely Bobby would be able to break the "barrier."

Two nights later in New York, Chicago suffered its third straight shutout, losing to the Rangers, 1–0.

Everyone thought the team had fallen to pieces under the pressure. The headline in one Chicago newspaper asked: "WILL THE HAWKS EVER SCORE AGAIN?"

Bobby's 51st goal was almost in sight on March 5,
when Toronto's Horton kept him from scoring.

The Chicago fans tried to help. They sent gifts to Bobby numbering "51" items.

He received 51 cans of tomato juice, 51 jars of jelly, 51 boxes of cereal, and 51 Kennedy half-dollars. A warehouse owner in Chicago gave Bobby 51 free days to store the merchandise he received.

There were 51 of everything, but there was no 51st goal.

On Saturday, March 12, 1966, the Black Hawks met the New York Rangers at Chicago Stadium. More than 20,000 fans jammed the arena.

Every eye followed Hull as he took the ice. Whenever he got the puck, the crowd screamed, "Go, Bobby, go!"

Through the first two periods of the game, the Black Hawks could not score. The Rangers meanwhile got two goals.

Not long after the third and final period had started, Hull picked up the puck and flicked a pass to Chico Maki, the Black Hawks' right wing. Maki banged it in.

Chicago's long streak of scoreless play had come to an end. The Black Hawks relaxed. Their spirit improved.

Less than three minutes later Hull got the puck. He swung toward center ice and

Hull slams in the 51st and hockey history is made!

into Ranger territory. He wound up, and with a mighty swing he slammed the black disk right by the New York goalie.

The stands went wild. Hats, gloves, paper cups, and plates—everything—came sailing down onto the ice. The great outburst of cheers, whistles, horns, and cowbells seemed to lift the roof. "I never heard so much noise before in all my life," Bobby said.

Bobby received many wonderful awards over the next few days. The nicest gift of

all came from three boys. They made 51 wooden pucks and numbered them from 1 to 51. Forty-nine of the pucks were painted black. The 50th was silver, and the 51st was gold.

After his ninth season of play with the Black Hawks, Bobby had rung up a total of 319 goals. He was the first player in hockey history to make more than 250 goals in fewer than 10 seasons of play.

On January 7, 1968, Bobby scored his

Keeping Hull in check is the best way to beat the Black Hawks. Bobby (above) is shadowed by a Ranger and (below) leaves his guard sprawling on the ice.

400th goal. Very few players have ever achieved this record.

How many goals will he have scored when he decides to retire? With Bobby Hull, almost any figure is possible.

Hull's amazing personal success has grown as he has put forth extraordinary efforts for his team. During the 60 minutes of actual play in each game, he has usually been on the ice about ten minutes longer than any other player. In addition to his regular turn at playing, he has taken on two additional duties.

He has been a vital part of Chicago's "power play," the attempt to score while the opposing team is at less than full strength. The Black Hawks, like all hockey teams, use the power play when the enemy team must send a man off the ice to the penalty box.

In the Chicago power play, Hull would

position himself about 60 feet from the opponent's net. With his teammates constantly feeding him the puck, Hull would fire shot after shot at the opposition goal. "He's like a piece of field artillery," said one player.

Hull has also served as one of his team's "penalty killers." He would go out on the ice whenever the Black Hawks lost a man to the penalty box so that he could help break up the foe's power play. By so doing, he helped "kill" his team's penalty minutes.

After the hockey season each year, Bobby, his wife, and their three young sons—Brett, Blake, and Bobby Jr.—return to their farm in southern Ontario. Hull has taken great pride in raising prize cattle on the farm. "I could never be a city boy," he once said.

The people of Point Anne have never forgotten Bobby Hull. The first thing one

The Hull family at home on their farm. Bobby hopes to retire here someday.

sees on visiting the town is a huge red, white, and blue sign. It reads:

POINT ANNE, BIRTHPLACE OF BOBBY HULL, THE WORLD'S GREATEST HOCKEY PLAYER

No one has raised any argument with Point Anne's description of Bobby Hull.

Howie Morenz,
the Stratford Streak

It was a crisp winter afternoon in 1920 in the Canadian town of Stratford. More than a thousand townspeople had gathered at the outdoor rink to watch their hockey team play a Montreal squad.

A slim youth with black hair and shining eyes scooped up the puck. In a few long, easy strides he reached lightning speed. Faster and faster he drove as he neared the enemy goal.

His shot was so hard that the puck was a black blur. The goalkeeper made a desperate lunge at it. Too late! The "Stratford Streak" had scored again.

"He's like an express train," said a man to a fan standing next to him. "Nothing can stop him. Who is that?"

"You must be kidding," said the fan. "Everyone around here knows. That man is Howie Morenz."

Before long all of Canada and the United States, too, would know the name of Howie Morenz.

The ice burned beneath his flying skates. He could overtake an enemy puck carrier, steal the black disk away, and be headed in the opposite direction before the other players quite knew what had happened. "When that guy skates at full speed," an opponent once said, "everyone else seems to be skating backward."

Morenz was not big for a hockey player. He was only five feet, nine inches tall. He weighed 165 pounds. When a pair of defensemen blocked his path, he would hurl his body into the air like a broad jumper to explode his way through. This type of charge became Morenz's trademark.

For the ten years beginning in 1923, Morenz was the outstanding player in the National Hockey League. He led the league in goals scored and in assists in the 1927–1928 season. He was awarded the Hart Trophy as the league's Most Valuable Player three times—in 1928, 1931, and 1932.

Howie Morenz was born in Mitchell, Ontario, a tiny town about 100 miles west of Toronto, on June 21, 1902. He was christened Howarth, not Howard. He was the youngest boy in a family of six children.

When he was seven, Howie was given his first pair of skates. They had belonged to

his older brother, Ezra, and were a bit large for Howie. He stuffed paper in the toes to make them fit.

The finest place to skate in Mitchell was the River Thames. On weekends and whenever school was not in session, the boys of the town would gather there to play hockey.

Except for their skates, the youngsters of Mitchell had very little "store-bought" equipment. Each team's goal was built of stones. The puck was a piece of coal. And each boy made his own hockey stick from a broom handle.

Howie was chunky as a boy and not as fast and strong as his older brothers. They did not want him on the attacking line, where speed and power counted. They made him play goalie. Howie could not afford to buy goalie pads, so he tucked a magazine into each stocking to protect his shins. When he was not playing hockey, he was practicing speed skating. He aspired, above all else, to skate fast.

Howie's father, who worked for the Canadian National Railway, encouraged the boy's interest in sports. But Howie's mother wanted him to become a musician.

She arranged for Howie to take piano lessons on Saturday mornings. To get to the piano teacher's home, Howie had to cross the River Thames. Passing the spirited action on the ice made him heartsick.

After two weeks of piano lessons, Howie could stand it no longer. He decided to skip the next lesson. He left his skates at a friend's house. That Saturday morning, instead of going to the piano lesson, he picked up his skates from his friend and joined the hockey game.

When he returned home in the afternoon, he headed directly for the family piano. He knew only one exercise, but he practiced it over and over.

After several weeks of listening to the very same exercise, Howie's mother became troubled. Her son did not seem to be learning anything new. She went to see the piano teacher.

"I came to inquire about my son Howie's lack of progress," said Mrs. Morenz. "When is he going to learn another exercise?"

The piano teacher gave her a puzzled look. "Howie?" she asked. "Howie who?"

Howie's mother then realized that a career in music was not her son's ambition.

Meanwhile Howie continued working hard to develop his skating speed. The practice began to pay dividends. His brothers let him move into the attacking line. When he was thirteen, Howie joined the Mitchell Juveniles and helped that team win the Western Ontario Juvenile championship.

A year later the Morenz family moved to Stratford, a city not far from Mitchell. There the flashing speed that he had developed won for Howie a position with the Stratford Seniors, an adult team.

Howie was touchy about his small size, so he was often involved in fist-swinging contests. One night after a bitter brawl on the ice, a friendly referee named Lou Marsh took Howie aside.

"Listen, kid," he said, "you're letting all those big guys make a fool of you. Don't

let them get you mad. Don't fight them."

"What else can I do?" Howie asked.

"Let them get the penalties," Marsh said. "You be the one that gets the goals."

When he was sixteen, Howie went to work in the railroad machine shop with his father. In his spare time he played amateur hockey for the railway team. He was the team's center in the attacking line between the two wingmen.

One night when their team went to Montreal for a game, Howie scored nine goals. That feat made him the talk of the hockey world. Several professional clubs wanted him to join their teams.

The Toronto St. Patricks—later known as the Maple Leafs—offered Howie $1,000 to play only five games. The Montreal Canadians said they would pay him $2,500 to play the full 24-game season of 1923–1924. These were "big money" offers then.

But Howie's parents did not want him to give up his job. "You've got security with the railroad," his mother told him. "Hockey is a foolish risk."

Howie agreed. Anyway he didn't think he was good enough. He knew he could skate fast now, but he believed any "pro" could skate faster.

In the spring of 1923, the Montreal club sent a special representative to Stratford to talk with Howie's father. The man's name was Cecil Hart.

"My son is not interested in becoming a professional," said Howie's father. "He's happy here."

"But let us sign him for just one year," Hart urged. "If he doesn't like us, we'll let him sell his services to another team. And if he doesn't like professional hockey, he can return to his railroad job."

Mr. Morenz signed the contract. Howie

himself could not sign. He had not yet reached the legal age of twenty-one.

Montreal club officials gathered at the team's training camp to watch Howie's first workout. When he came onto the ice, with only three or four quick strides he was sailing at full speed.

Leo Dandurand, the owner of the team, watched Howie make a full circle of the ice. Then he walked over to Cecil Hart. He put his hand on Hart's shoulder and said, "Cecil, the Lord had you in his arms when you signed that boy."

Montreal had a magnificent team that sparkled with stars. Howie felt out of place when he went on the ice with them. Then he discovered that he could outskate any man on the team. His doubts about his skills began to disappear.

One day during the training season, Cecil Hart motioned Howie aside. "We've been watching you carefully," he said. "We want you to be the team's starting center."

As a rookie player, Howie scored 13 goals in that 24-game season of 1923–1924. His team won the Stanley Cup, the award given to the champion team at the end of the season. Winning the Stanley Cup in hockey is like winning the World Series in baseball or the Super Bowl game in pro football.

Sportswriters had several nicknames for Howie. Each was a tribute to his blazing speed. Besides calling him the "Stratford Streak," they dubbed him the "Mitchell Meteor," the "Canadian Comet," and the "Phantom of the Ice."

Sometimes no one could prevent Morenz from putting the puck in the net. One night in a game against the Toronto Maple Leafs, Conn Smythe, the Toronto coach, assigned a 210-pound defenseman named Bert Corbeau to handle Morenz.

"I don't care how you do it, just stop him," Smythe ordered.

The first time Howie swept down the ice, Corbeau was waiting with a body check. He caught Morenz with a hip and sent him flying.

As Morenz hit the ice, Corbeau grinned and yelled over to the Toronto bench: "How's that, coach? How's that for stopping him?"

"Look behind you!" Smythe barked.

Morenz, at the instant he was hit, had fired a shot at the Toronto goal—and the shot was good!

Newspapermen also called Morenz "Hurtling Howie," describing Howie's habit of throwing himself at enemy defensemen.

This tactic was not always successful. One night when the Canadiens were playing the Boston Bruins, the Bruins faced Morenz with two of the best defensemen of

the day, Eddie Shore and Lionel Hitchman. Both were big and rugged bruisers.

Whenever Howie brought the puck down the ice, these two were waiting for him with a special body-check strategy. Shore would drive Howie toward his partner. Hitchman would bull into Howie with shoulder or hip to send him sprawling.

Four times that evening Howie charged. Four times Shore and Hitchman butted him

to the ice. But Howie was plotting his own counter-strategy.

The next time the Canadiens and Bruins met, Shore and Hitchman got set to give Howie another one-two treatment. When Morenz got the puck, he whizzed straight for the pair. Shore moved to nudge Howie into the waiting Hitchman.

But he never did get the chance. Howie roared to within inches of Shore, suddenly swerved, then skated around both Shore and Hitchman to score a goal.

The next time and every time thereafter, when the Canadiens faced the Bruins, Shore and Hitchman treated Morenz with more caution.

On many other occasions during his career, Morenz was the object of violence. But he never reacted with violence. Howie seemed to save all his fight for the game. He had learned his lesson from Lou Marsh.

Once when the Canadiens were playing the Ottawa Senators, Howie was involved in a fierce collision with Hector Kilrea of the Ottawa team. Kilrea, believing that the crash was Howie's fault, struck Howie across the head with his stick. The blow knocked Howie unconscious.

Howie was carried to the Montreal dressing room. After a long time, he opened his eyes.

"Was that Kilrea that hit me?" Morenz asked.

"Yes, it was," a newspaperman answered.

"With his stick?" Howie asked.

The newspaperman nodded.

"Well, I know Hec," Morenz said softly. "I don't think he meant to do it."

In the 1929–30 season, Howie scored 40 goals. In those days a team averaged 44 games in a season. Today each team plays 74 games. Howie's goals had come at the fantastic rate of almost one per game.

The Canadiens won the Stanley Cup in 1930 and again in 1931. But in 1932 the Toronto Maple Leafs won it.

Even though he was only thirty, Howie appeared to be slowing down. His muscles and reflexes were paying the price for the years of fierce play and the various injuries he had suffered. And Howie had always lived just as he played—to the fullest. It was no secret that he had broken training rules.

Statistics tell the story. In the 1932–1933 season, Howie scored only fourteen goals. The next season his total dropped to eight.

His old doubts about his ability returned. Then one night Howie heard his Montreal fans boo him. His confidence was shattered.

In 1934 the Canadiens traded him to the Chicago Black Hawks. Morenz broke down and cried when he learned that his beloved Canadiens were letting him go. He knew he had to report to his new team or risk being suspended from the league. Suspension would put an end to his hockey career, and hockey was life itself to Howie.

But Howie's career kept going downhill. He missed his friends in Montreal. He missed the city itself. When he failed to produce goals for the Black Hawks, the team traded him to the New York Rangers.

Howie was in the depths of discouragement.

Then a group of new owners took over the Canadiens in 1936. The previous owners had let Cecil Hart go, as well as Howie, but the new group brought Hart back. Hart remembered Howie's years of glory, and he knew of Howie's present despair. Hart quickly worked a trade with the Rangers to bring Howie back to Montreal.

Hart made Howie his special project. "I expect you to set an example for the younger players," Hart told him. Hart's use of psychology worked. Howie became the first player to arrive at practice sessions and the last one to leave. His spirit began to revive.

Then Hart made Howie the team's starting center. "You can do it," he said. "The team's counting on you."

Morenz began a thrilling comeback. His old speed returned. The fans cheered him

as they had before. Early in the 1936–1937 season, the Canadiens captured first place in league standings, thanks to Howie's heroic play.

On the night of January 28, 1937, the Canadiens were playing the Chicago Black Hawks. Morenz got the puck. He raced right for the Chicago defensemen in typical fashion. As Morenz leaped into the air, he tripped over a stick and smashed into the boards that lined the rink. The crash broke his leg in three places.

"I'm all through, I'm finished," Morenz gasped after he had been taken to the dressing room.

For weeks Howie lay in a hospital bed, his leg encased in a heavy cast. Every waking moment was darkened by the conviction that he would never play hockey again. Late in February Howie suffered an attack of pneumonia. His friends said he would fight it off, just as he would fight to score a goal. Then they realized that the Canadian Meteor could not fight. Early in March of that year Howie died, leaving behind an unequaled career in the world of hockey.

Maurice Richard, the Rocket

Newspapers gave the explosive Maurice Richard (pronounced *Ree-shar*) the perfect nickname. They called him the "Rocket."

Like any rocket, this one had plenty of firepower.

One night Richard's team, the Montreal Canadiens, faced the Detroit Red Wings. Richard was sent to the penalty box for using rough tactics. He sat gloomily as the Red Wings scored twice and took a 2–0 lead.

When his penalty time had been served, Richard leaped from the bench and streaked out onto the ice. He gathered in a loose puck, broke through the Detroit defenses, and fired a sizzling shot past the Red Wings' goalie.

Not more than a minute later, Elmer Lach, one of the Rocket's teammates, had control of the puck. He sailed a pass across the ice to Maurice.

The Rocket was off again. He swooped in on the net at breakneck speed. This shot was a quick backhand. It was perfect.

As Maurice skated up the ice, Dick Irvin, the Montreal coach, waved him over to the sidelines. "You'd better take a rest," Irvin said. "You're going to burn yourself out."

The Rocket grinned. "I had my rest in the penalty box," he said. "Let me stay on the ice."

Irvin nodded to Richard. "O.K.," he said.

Lach had the puck again. He slid a pass to Hector "Toe" Blake. Then Blake passed to Richard.

The Rocket roared down the ice again. A Detroit defenseman moved to stop him, but Richard bowled him over. The shot was high and hard—and good!

The screaming fans could hardly believe what they had seen. The Rocket had scored three goals in less than three minutes. He was a one-man team. The final score read Montreal 3, Detroit 2.

It is doubtful if ice hockey has ever seen the likes of Maurice Richard. He was a strong and fast skater, a deadly accurate shooter, and during the 1950's had no equal as a goal-getter.

He is remembered for great skill and many records, but most of all he is remembered for his fiery spirit.

The Rocket scores past Boston's Red Henry.

The Rocket could not bear to lose. He would go to any lengths to put the puck in the enemy net.

Once in a game against the Detroit Red Wings, the Rocket got the puck and raced down the ice. Nearing the Detroit goal, he saw that Earl Seibert, a rugged 220-pound defenseman, was blocking his path.

Moving at top speed, the Rocket bent low, then met Seibert in a head-on crash.

After the collision Maurice kept his balance and got his shot away—with Seibert atop his shoulders!

Maurice Richard was born on August 4, 1921, in the city of Montreal. He was the oldest of eight children.

Maurice's mother and father were French-Canadians. Only French was spoken in the Richard home. Maurice played with French-speaking children and attended French schools. He heard very little English until he became a major league hockey player.

Young Maurice was a natural athlete. He was a fine boxer and wrestler, and a splendid outfielder in baseball and softball.

Hockey, however, is the great love of every sportsminded Canadian youngster. Maurice was no different from the others.

The *Rivière des Prairies*, which flows to the north and west of Montreal, becomes a broad sheet of windswept ice each winter.

Here Maurice learned how to skate and play hockey.

Maurice had long jet-black hair, which he combed straight back, and dark deep-set eyes. He was of average height and weight. From skating over the great open surface of the river, he developed legs and arms of steel.

He learned to make good use of his strength. When he carried the puck on the end of his stick, he used his powerful left arm like a battering ram to ward off opposing players.

"He's as strong as an ox," said one opponent. "When he gets his body between you and the puck, you're finished."

Off the ice young Maurice was quiet and shy. But as soon as he laced on his skates, he became bold and aggressive.

While he was in school, Maurice joined a junior hockey team that represented one of the city's parks. The manager of the hockey team was named Jacques Fontaine. Once when the team needed skates and uniforms, Jacques wrote to the Montreal Canadiens and asked for a donation to help the team buy equipment.

The Canadiens sent Jacques the money that the team needed.

Jacques was very grateful. He wrote to the Montreal team once again. "Within five years," he promised, "I will send you a hockey player. A good one."

Jacques kept his promise. In the winter of 1940, a skinny twenty-year-old youngster presented himself at the office of Tommy Gorman, the manager of the Montreal Canadiens.

"I'm Maurice Richard," he said shyly. "Jacques Fontaine sent me."

Gorman was puzzled. Several years had passed since the Canadiens had received

Jacques' letter, and the promise had been forgotten.

"I'm here to play hockey for your team," Maurice explained.

Gorman grinned. He liked Maurice. He admired the confidence he had. Gorman had a hunch that this young man might become a star one day. He decided to give him a try.

"Go and see our coach, Dick Irvin," Gorman said. "He'll get you a uniform and arrange for a tryout."

The day of the tryout finally came. Coach Irvin planned to test Maurice's courage. He spoke to Murph Chamberlain, a veteran player known for his rough and tough play. "See if this kid can take it," Irvin ordered.

From the moment play began, the rugged Chamberlain hammered poor Maurice with a steady rain of hips, elbows, and knees.

Maurice could take only so much. Suddenly he flung his stick to the ice, threw off his gloves, and attacked Chamberlain with flying fists. It took three players to pull him away. No one ever tested Maurice's ability to take it again.

Gorman sent Maurice to an amateur team to get more playing experience. Maurice had a hard time. In his first game he broke his left ankle. He did not play any more that season. He got a job in a machine shop.

The next year Maurice broke his left wrist playing hockey. "Your bones may be too brittle for ice hockey," the doctor told him. "They're just like peppermint sticks." Maurice was beginning to believe he was destined for a career as a machinist.

But the Montreal team still felt that Maurice could be a great player. In the fall of 1942, they invited him to come to their training camp. He looked so good that they signed him to a contract to play for the Canadiens.

In a game against the Boston Bruins, Maurice skated into a hard body check thrown by Johnny Crawford, a Boston defenseman. He spun off Crawford and crashed into the sideboards. Another broken ankle was the result.

Coach Irvin came to Maurice with some

sad advice. "I think you should think about quitting the game," he said. "I don't think you can make it."

Maurice would not give up, however. He went to see manager Tommy Gorman and begged for just one more chance. Gorman could not refuse. He told Maurice to come back the following season.

During training season the next fall, Coach Irvin decided to try Maurice on a new attacking line. Maurice was to play right wing, Toe Blake would play left wing, and Elmer Lach would be the center.

This combination was to become one of the most dangerous in hockey history. It was called the "Punch Line." Maurice remained in good health, and the "Punch Line" earned nearly every scoring record.

They managed to do this even though the players who made up the line had a language problem. Elmer Lach spoke only

English. The Rocket spoke only French. Toe Blake, however, could speak both of these languages.

Not being able to speak English caused Maurice hardly any difficulty when he was on the ice. "I just did what was natural for me, and the plays worked out," he once said. "Hockey has a language all its own."

But the Rocket did start to learn English soon after he joined the Montreal team in 1942. Within a few seasons he spoke the language almost as well as though it had been his native tongue.

During the 1944–45 season, the Rocket's third year with the Montreal team, he scored 50 goals. This was an amazing record, for the previous high score was 43.

This record was set during World War II. Some critics said that the Rocket was helped by weak opposition. They predicted that when the league's "big guns" returned

Richard and two teammates try desperately to get at the puck under a Ranger player in a 1944 game.

from the armed services, Richard's scoring total would drop. Maurice himself had been rejected by the Army because of disability resulting from previous injuries.

The critics were wrong. The "name" players returned, but they could not stop the Rocket. In the 1948–1949 season, he was again the league's leading goal getter.

The Rocket set his record during a season that was only 50 games in length. No one else has equaled his record in 50 games. A few other players have tallied 50 goals but they have done so during 70 to 74 game seasons.

People never knew when the Rocket was going to explode. One December night in 1944, he came into the Canadiens' dressing room and slumped down on a bench.

"Don't depend on me too much tonight," he said. "I'm bushed."

"You do look tired," said a teammate. "How come?"

"This afternoon we moved to a new apartment, and I couldn't hire a truck," Maurice answered. "My brother and I carried all the furniture on our backs."

That night in a game against the Detroit Red Wings, the Rocket broke the league scoring record. He netted five goals, and made three assists for a total of eight points. The record has been tied once since but never beaten.

After the game Coach Irvin clapped Maurice on the back. "Nice going," he said, "but what would you have done if you hadn't been tired?"

Richard's goal-scoring ability won him many honors. He was named to the league's All-Star team eight times. In 1947 he was voted the Hart Trophy as the National Hockey League's Most Valuable Player.

The Richard home in Montreal contains trophies of almost every size and description. One prize, however, that is not in his collection is the Lady Byng Trophy. This is the National Hockey League award for "sportsmanship and gentlemanly conduct."

The Rocket often used his fists during the heat of battle. He was frequently sent to the penalty box because of rough play. During his career he paid more than $3,000 in fines for disobeying good conduct rules.

But Maurice seldom started a scrap. He only used his fists or swung his stick on those who had struck him first.

"I never criticize the Rocket for blowing up and socking people," Dick Irvin once stated. "After all, he's the most illegally

Despite heavy guarding, the Rocket (9) slams in a goal past New York's Rayner in a 1949 game.

held, pushed, battered, and elbowed man in the league."

A team often would assign a man the full-time job of preventing the Rocket from scoring. Because he must stay so close to the man he is guarding, a player on such an assignment is called a "shadow."

Tony Leswick of the New York Rangers was a shadow. In one game against the New York team, the Rocket snared a loose puck and headed for the Rangers' goal. Leswick grabbed Richard's jersey, but the Rocket kept moving at jet-plane speed.

Then Leswick rammed his stick into Richard's ribs. As if that were not enough, Gus Kyle, another Ranger, slammed into the Rocket with a terrific body check.

Richard fell to the ice. Kyle landed on top of him. Leswick landed on top of Kyle.

Somehow the Rocket got his stick free and managed a powerful swing at the

Sometimes it's a miss! Ranger Lorne Worsley
lunges at Richard's shot (above) and manages
to push it aside as the Rocket charges in.

puck. It sailed into an unprotected corner of the net.

Chuck Rayner, the New York goalie, boiled with rage. "Why didn't you hold him, Tony?" Rayner barked.

"What do you want me to do," Leswick answered, "tie him up?"

One day in 1955 Maurice appeared in the office of Frank Selke, managing director of the Canadiens. He had his younger brother, Henri, with him. Henri, who was only nine-teen, was somewhat smaller than Maurice. He had played junior hockey as center.

"My brother Henri wants to play for the Canadiens," Maurice announced.

Mr. Selke replied that he didn't believe Henri was ready for major league play. "Another year's experience in a junior league might be good for him," he said.

Maurice protested. "He doesn't want to be a junior any more," he declared. "He's good enough now to play for the Canadiens." Henri nodded in agreement.

Few people had ever been able to oppose Maurice successfully, on or off the ice. Resisting *two* Richards was impossible. Mr. Selke agreed to give Henri a tryout. Soon after, he signed the younger brother to a contract.

As the two brothers were leaving Mr. Selke's office, Maurice made a prediction. "Mr. Selke," he said, "long after I retire, Henri will still be playing hockey for the Montreal Canadiens."

Maurice was right. Henri became one of the brightest stars in Montreal history and continued to play for many years after his older brother retired.

Toe Blake became the Montreal coach in 1955. He decided to use Maurice and Henri in the same attacking line. Maurice took his regular post at right wing.

Henri (left) and Maurice Richard lace up their
skates in the Canadiens' dressing room.

The "Richard Line" in action in 1956—the Rocket,
with an assist from Henri (left), scores.

The "Richard Line," as it was called,
ranked as the most powerful of its day.
The Canadiens won the Stanley Cup in
1955–1956 and 1956–1957, the first two
seasons the Richard Line was used.

The next season, in a game against
Toronto, Maurice was hurt in a smash-up
with another player. As he fell to the ice,
someone's skate blade accidentally cut the

Achilles' tendon in the back of his right heel.

This injury can be a disaster for a hockey player. A tendon is a piece of tough tissue that connects muscle fiber to the bones. Without a sound Achilles' tendon, a skater cannot swerve or stop short. He cannot produce power or speed.

Maurice had to miss many weeks of play. Rumors spread that the Rocket wouldn't ever play hockey again. But an operation repaired the damage.

Late in the season Maurice did return to play. In his first appearance he slammed home two goals. The next night he scored two more.

In the playoffs that year, he left no doubt that he had regained his brilliant touch. He scored eleven goals, only one less than his all-time record for a playoff year. He was the driving force that helped the Canadiens secure their third straight Stanley Cup title in 1957–1958.

One of the goals he scored during the playoffs became a famous example of the Rocket's dauntless will to win.

The Canadiens were playing the Detroit Red Wings. The Rocket had the puck and came skimming down the ice past the Detroit defensemen.

He bore down on the goalkeeper and shot. But at the moment he fired, a Detroit player grabbed the Rocket around the waist and toppled him to the ice. The puck dribbled harmlessly off the end of his stick.

The Rocket rose to one knee and took a desperate jab at the puck. His aim was perfect. The black disk sailed right by the astonished goalie.

Maurice had scored from many positions, but this was the first time he had ever scored while kneeling.

**Team Captain Maurice Richard and the Canadiens'
coach Toe Blake display the Stanley Cup in 1957.**

After the game a newspaper reporter
asked Jack Adams, the manager of the
Red Wings, if he knew any way to stop
the Rocket.

Adams thought for a minute. "There's
really only one way," he said. "With a
gun."

The Canadiens won the Stanley Cup in

1958–1959 season and again in 1959–1960 for their fifth straight championship. It was a feat no other team had achieved in all of hockey history.

In the 1959–1960 season, the Rocket scored 19 goals, giving him a career total of 544 goals. This, too, established a record in hockey history.

His teammates and the fans expected Richard to play at least one or two seasons more. But the Rocket knew he was slowing down. In September 1960 he announced he was retiring as a player.

Everyone asked, "Why?"

George "Punch" Imlach, manager and coach of the Toronto Maple Leafs, had the answer.

"The Rocket has never been content to be just good," he said. "He has always wanted to be the best. He wouldn't settle for anything else."

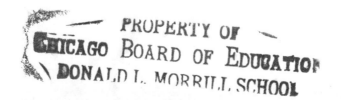